MIRACLE MAKER

A life of Jesus,
retold and remembered

Retold and compiled by Mary Joslin

Illustrated by Francesca Pelizzoli

A LION BOOK

For Mum & Dad
with thanks N.J.
For Simon & Sophia
F.P.

Book design by Nicky Jex
Text by Mary Joslin
Illustrations copyright © 1998 Francesca Pelizzoli
This edition copyright © 1998 Lion Publishing

The author asserts the moral right
to be identified as the author of this work

Published by
Lion Publishing plc
Sandy Lane West, Oxford, England
ISBN 0 7459 3629 6

First edition 1998
10 9 8 7 6 5 4 3 2 1 0

Acknowledgments
Bible passages quoted or adapted from the
Good News Bible published by the Bible
Societies/HarperCollins Publishers Ltd UK
© American Bible Society
1996, 1992, 1976, 1971

A catalogue record for this book is available
from the British Library

Printed and bound in Spain

Introduction

The story of Jesus is the story of a man who worked miracles.

He healed the sick.

He fed the hungry.

Thousands came to see if the amazing stories they had heard of his doings were true.

There were other miracles, too. He inspired people to change the way they lived… to become more generous, more forgiving, and to find joy in so doing.

It was surely by a miracle that Jesus forgave his enemies, who hunted him down and had him put to death; it was by an even greater miracle that he rose to life again, as his followers so firmly believed he did.

Certainly, something happened to Jesus' friends in the days and weeks after they saw him publicly crucified; something enabled them to conquer their fear and come out of hiding;

something gave them the courage to go into all the world and tell people of Jesus' life and his message of healing, forgiveness and love.

The miracle of Jesus has continued for two thousand years. Many people who hear his story find themselves changed by it… find themselves inspired by his example of selfless love, of wholehearted compassion, and of trust in God in good times and in bad.

Many of these people have, in their turn, retold the story of Jesus, to show others how it has become part of the story of their own transformed lives.

Here is a glimpse of that great story… that unfolding miracle.

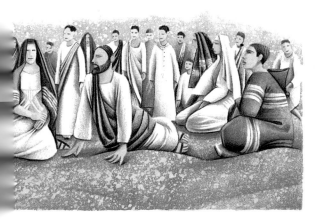

Contents

Longing for a Miracle

*Long ago, on the shores of a lake named Galilee,
country folk lived plain, hardworking lives.*

Life in Galilee

Many of the people who lived in Galilee were farmers. They tilled the thin soil on the rocky hillsides, sowing seeds in spring and in summer reaping the golden barley for the good grain that was ground into bread. They tended sprawling vines, where bunches of luscious grapes ripened in the early autumn and the sweet juice was made into wine. On ancient olive trees the green fruit slowly turned a deep, rich black as the year drew to a close, and children beat the branches to make the olives fall to the ground.

Other Galilee folk looked after flocks of sheep and goats. In the day they led their flocks out to the hillsides to find grass and herbs to nibble. At night, they gathered the animals into low-walled sheepfolds.

Yet others fished for a living: they took their little boats onto the violet-blue lake that nestled among the hills and dragged their nets through the water in the hope of making a good catch to sell on the shore.

In amongst the working people, children laughed and played. When the sun shone bright and golden, life seemed good and full of promise.

Yet how quickly the world could turn dark: when storm winds blew and seemed to call up terrifying forces of chaos from the depths of the lake water, or when ragged black clouds flapped across the night sky like great, shadowy birds.

Or when people thought about the bleakness of their lives: the disappointments, the sorrows, the burden of paying heavy taxes to their Roman overlords, the brutality of the Roman soldiers who patrolled their land on behalf of a pagan emperor.

Then the people set to wondering: had their God abandoned them? What of the promises in their ancient scriptures… that God would send them a king greater than the greatest kings of old… a Messiah… a Christ… a king who would rescue them from their troubles?

God's Great Promise

'The people who walked in darkness have seen a great light. They lived in a land of shadows, but now light is shining on them.

You have given them great joy, Lord; you have made them happy…

A child is born to us!

A son is given to us!

And he will be our ruler.

He will be called "Wonderful Counsellor", "Mighty God", "Eternal Father", "Prince of Peace".

His royal power will continue to grow; his kingdom will always be at peace.

He will rule as King David's successor, basing his power on right and justice, from now until the end of time.'

Isaiah 9:2–3, 6–7

Lord of the Winds

Lord of the winds, I cry to thee,
I that am dust,
And blown about by every gust
I fly to thee.

Lord of the waters, unto thee I call.
I that am weed upon the waters borne,
And by the waters torn,
Tossed by the waters, at thy feet I fall.

Mary Coleridge (1861–1907)

The Miracle Birth

In the hills around Lake Galilee stood the plainest and most ordinary of little towns: Nazareth. And in that very ordinary place lived a young woman named Mary. She was looking forward to getting married, just like the other girls of her age.

Her family had chosen a husband for her: Joseph, a good man from a respectable family and an honest carpenter.
Then something quite extraordinary happened.

A Greeting from an Angel

God sent the angel Gabriel to a town in Galilee named Nazareth. The angel had a message for a girl promised in marriage to a man named Joseph, who was a descendant of the nation's great King David. The girl's name was Mary. The angel came to her and said, 'Peace be with you! The Lord is with you and has greatly blessed you!'

Mary was deeply troubled by the angel's message, and she wondered what the words meant. The angel noticed the fear and wonder in her eyes, and spoke again.

'Don't be afraid, Mary,' the angel said, 'God has been gracious to you. You will become pregnant and give birth to a son, and you will name him Jesus. He will be great and will be called the Son of the Most High God.'

Mary was practical and was perplexed. 'How can I have a baby?' she asked. 'I'm not even a wife yet, so how can I become a mother?'

The angel's reply was simple: 'God's power will make it happen.'

Mary bowed her head a moment to think. She had been brought up to live by God's laws. Now she was older, that was what she herself wanted to do. If this message was truly from God, then she knew what her answer must be. 'I am the Lord's servant,' said Mary; 'may it happen to me as you have said.'

And the angel left her.

Retold from Luke 1:26–38

Mary Visits a Friend

Mary could scarcely believe what the angel had said. To whom could she tell her strange but exciting secret? She decided to confide in her cousin Elizabeth—a woman much older than Mary, and a good and kind friend. Surprisingly, she too was expecting a baby…

Almost before she heard the news, Elizabeth was filled with joy and delight. 'You are the most blessed of all women,' she exclaimed, 'and blessed is the child you will bear!'

When Mary realized what a great honour was hers, a song of joy welled up within her.

She sang, 'My heart praises the Lord; my soul is glad because of God my Saviour, for he has remembered me, his lowly servant! From now on all people will call me blessed, because of the great things the Mighty God has done for me. Holy is his name…'

Retold from Luke 1:39–49

The Angel Gabriel

The angel Gabriel from heaven came,
His wings as drifted snow, his eyes as flame;
'All hail,' said he, 'thou lowly maiden Mary,
'Most highly favoured lady.'
Gloria!

'For know a blessèd mother thou shalt be,
'All generations laud and honour thee,
'Thy son shall be Emmanuel, by seers foretold.
'Most highly favoured lady.'
Gloria!

Then gentle Mary meekly bowed her head.
'To me be as it pleaseth God,' she said,
'My soul shall laud and magnify his holy name.'
Most highly favoured lady.
Gloria!

Of her, Emmanuel, the Christ, was born
In Bethlehem, all on a Christmas morn,
And Christian folk throughout the world will ever say,
'Most highly favoured lady.'
Gloria!

S. Baring-Gould (1834–1924)

Jesus is Born

When Mary announced she was pregnant, Joseph was dismayed. How could he marry her if she was expecting someone else's baby? Then he had a dream and something in it reassured him. He agreed to take care of Mary and the baby.

At that time, a man named Caesar Augustus ruled the mighty Roman Empire. He wanted to know exactly how many people he ruled, so that he could demand taxes from them. Everyone had to go to the town their family came from and register their names. Joseph had to travel from Nazareth in Galilee to Bethlehem, many miles to the south. It was just a little hilltop town; yet no one had ever forgotten that the nation's great King David had been born there, almost a thousand years earlier.

Retold from Matthew 2:18–24 and Luke 2:1–4

The Weary Travellers

Mary was heavily pregnant now, her young body big and cumbersome and, oh, so weary from the long journey. Then the cramping pains of labour were upon her… It seemed certain that her baby was going to be born while she was far away from home: here, in Bethlehem. 'Oh Joseph, Joseph,' she cried. 'We have travelled so far, and need a place to stay; yet now you tell me all the rooms for travellers are full. Whatever shall we do?'

Joseph was not dismayed. Months earlier, in a dream, an angel had told him to take care of Mary and her baby. He must now do what he thought best… and trust God that all would be well. 'Mary, dear Mary,' he replied, 'here is a stable where we can shelter. There is clean straw, enough room to lie down, and the cold night breezes cannot chill us.'

There, among the animals, Jesus was born. Mary wrapped her baby warmly in swaddling clothes. Joseph piled straw into an ancient stone manger, to make it into a cradle. There, Mary laid her baby.

Retold from Luke 2:4–7 amd Matthew 1:18–21

A Message from Heaven

That same night, on the hillsides sloping down from Bethlehem, some shepherds were out looking after their flocks. It was dull, tedious work sitting out in the cold night air, listening for the sounds of danger... the sniffing of prowling animals, the stealthy footsteps of thieves and robbers...

But what was this? A sudden a blaze of brightness, a clear and glorious shining... a pure and lovely goodness but so, so terrifying. An angel... it had to be... an angel of God.

The angel said to them, 'Don't be afraid! I am here with good news for you, which will bring great joy to all people. This very day in David's town, your Saviour was born— Christ the Lord! And this is what will prove it to you: you will find a baby wrapped in strips of cloth and lying in a manger.'

Suddenly a great army of heaven's angels appeared, singing praises to God: 'Glory to God in the highest heaven, and peace on earth to those with whom he is pleased.'

Then the sky was dark again, miles and miles of dark hung with silver stars. The shepherds fell to wondering about what they had seen. Was it true, what the angels had said? Was a new light shining for their nation? Had God's promised king come to earth?

They hurried to Bethlehem. There they found Mary and the baby, just as the angel had said.

Retold from Luke 2:8–16

The Shepherds' Carol

We stood on the hills, Lady,
Our day's work done,
Watching the frosted meadows,
That winter had won.

The evening was calm, Lady,
The air so still,
Silence more lovely than music,
Folded the hill.

There was a star, Lady,
Shone in the night,
Larger than Venus it was
And bright, so bright.

Oh, a voice from the sky, Lady,
It seemed to us then
Telling of God being born
In the world of men.

And so we have come, Lady,
Our day's work done,
Our love, our hopes, ourselves
We give to your son.

Anonymous

Joy to the World

Not far from Bethlehem, in the nation's capital city of Jerusalem, a king named Herod sat and fretted. Every day seemed to bring a new threat to his power.

King Herod and the Wise Men

King Herod ruled his people on behalf of the Romans. He loved power. He had schemed to win it; he had plotted to keep it. He had killed for power… and he would kill again.

A party of travellers was now heading towards Jerusalem: scholars from lands to the East. They were following a star. 'We believe the star is a sign,' they told people in Jerusalem. 'We believe it is telling us that a new king has been born to the Jews. We have come to worship that king.'

King Herod had spies everywhere. King Herod wanted to know every last rumour of anyone who had ambitions to take his place. King Herod heard of their quest. And King Herod was afraid.

So he called together the scholars of his own people. 'Travellers have started rumours,' he hissed. 'People are beginning to whisper that God's great king has been born—the one our people call "Messiah" and the Greek speakers call "Christ". What do we know about that promise of a Messiah? Where will he be born?'

'Ah,' replied the scholars, 'the answer to that question is found among the holy books of our people. Long ago, a man of God named Micah said these words:

"Bethlehem, in the land of Judah, you are by no means the least of the great cities of Judah; for from you will come a leader who will guide the people of God, the people of Israel." '

Herod called the travellers to a secret meeting. 'Tell me all about the star you are following,' he said. 'I want to know exactly when it appeared in the sky.'

So they told him what they knew, and he told them to go to Bethlehem. 'Go and look for that king,' he said softly. Then his voice grew cold: 'When you have found him, come back and tell me where he is… so I can go and worship him too.'

The travellers left the palace. As they journeyed to Bethlehem, the star shone ahead of them. It hung right over one house. There they found Mary, and her newborn son.

They fell on their knees to worship him. They gave him rich gifts: gold, frankincense and myrrh.

Here, they believed, was the new king… a king for all the world.

Retold from Matthew 2:1–11 and Micah 5:2

What Can I Give Him?

What can I give him,
Poor as I am?
If I were a shepherd
I would bring a lamb;
If I were a wise man
I would do my part;
Yet what I can I give him—
Give my heart.

Christina Rossetti (1830–94)

Escape from Danger

When the learned men saw the baby Jesus they knew they had found the king they sought. But then something warned them that they must never tell Herod about the little boy. They went home to their country by a different road.

Joseph also suspected danger, having been warned about Herod in a dream. So he took his family to Egypt for a while, to keep them safe.

Retold from Matthew 2:12–15

A Child Among Us

At last, Joseph and Mary returned home to Nazareth in Galilee with Jesus. There, the little boy grew up with other children his age. As the years went by, he learned the way of life of his people—their customs, their beliefs, and their faith in God. He was a boy like other boys.

Among the Poor

Christ is merciful and mild:
He was once a little child:
He whom heavenly hosts adore
Lived on earth among the poor...

He, who is the Lord most high,
Then was poorer far than I,
That I might hereafter be
Rich to all eternity.

From *Gospel Hymns for Children*
(published in 1898)

A Story of Jesus' Boyhood

Every year Jesus' parents made the long journey from Nazareth to Jerusalem to celebrate the religious festival of their people known as Passover.

In Jerusalem, the Jewish people could worship at the Temple—the place that reminded them that God dwelt among them.

When Jesus was twelve years old, his parents took him to Jerusalem for the Passover festival. What a sight as they approached! The Temple stood on a hill, and it towered above the city walls, gleaming gold and white in the spring sunshine. Eager pilgrims streamed towards the city, and everyone was in a holiday mood. Within the Temple itself, solemn priests in white tunics and turbans were busy with the ceremonies, and Jesus was old enough to stand with the men, watching. All too soon, the holiday was over, and the group of pilgrims from Nazareth had to begin the long journey back home.

After one day's journey, Mary began to worry. She had not seen Jesus for hours. Where could he be? She began to ask among the other families, 'Have you seen Jesus recently?' 'Was he talking to your boy today?'

'Yes, we saw him yesterday too, but today...'

No one had seen him. No one at all. As the sky turned dark that night, it became clear that Jesus was not with the party.

Now Jesus' parents were truly alarmed. They must simply go back to Jerusalem and see if they could find him… hoping that he was safe, hoping that he hadn't fallen into bad company… or worse.

They searched the places where they had stayed. They questioned the traders in the street; they even spoke to beggars who sat at the corners and would readily provide answers for a coin or two—but nobody could help them.

On the third day they found Jesus. He was in the courtyard of the Temple, in the shady colonnade, listening to the Jewish teachers and asking questions. All who heard him were amazed at his intelligent answers.

His parents were astonished when they saw him, but after days of anxiety, anger took over. His mother marched over and broke into the conversation sharply: 'My son, why have you done this to us? Your father and I have been terribly worried trying to find you.'

When Jesus turned to look at her, she knew she was looking into the eyes of a young man.

He answered simply, 'Why did you have to look for me? Didn't you know that I had to be in my Father's house?' But they did not understand his answer.

Jesus went back with them to Nazareth, and was obedient to them. As time passed, Mary forgot her anxiety. She remembered instead the smiling admiration of the people in the Temple who had been talking with Jesus, her very special son, and she treasured all these memories in her heart.

Retold from Luke 2:41–51

13

The Miracle Worker

Jesus had a cousin named John who was just a few months older than him. When they were both grown-up, John became a wandering preacher. Like the prophets of ancient days, whose words were written in the scriptures, John dressed in rough cloth and ate the meagre food he could find in the sun-bleached wilderness.

Yet the things he said about God drew the crowds to listen to him.

He called people to change: to turn around on the path of selfishness and live as God wanted, loving God and other people. Those that wanted to do so he baptized, dipping them briefly in the River Jordan as a sign of their making a fresh start.

Jesus' New Beginning

One day, Jesus left Nazareth in Galilee to go and see his cousin John.

'Why do you want to be baptized?' asked John, amazed. 'You're a better person than I am—you should be baptizing me.'

But Jesus insisted. As soon as Jesus came up out of the water of the River Jordan, he saw heaven opening, and God's Spirit coming down on him like a dove. And a voice came from heaven, 'You are my dear Son. I am pleased with you.'

At once the Spirit made Jesus go into the desert, where he stayed for forty days. The Evil One, Satan, came and tempted him. The work that lay ahead of him was hard and dangerous. Easier paths beckoned. Yet there in the barren desert, among the wild animals, Jesus made up his mind to do what he felt God was calling him to do. And then he did not feel so alone… for angels came and helped him.

Retold from Mark 1:9–13 and Matthew 3:13–17

The Time has Come

Then Jesus returned to Galilee and began preaching and teaching, amazing all who heard him. One day, he went to the synagogue in Nazareth where he had been brought up. He was asked to read from the scriptures, so he unrolled the scroll and found these words in the book of the prophet Isaiah:

'The Spirit of the Lord is upon me, because he has chosen me to bring good news to the poor. He has sent me to proclaim liberty to the captives and recovery of sight to the blind; to set free the oppressed and announce that the time has come when the Lord will save his people.'

Jesus added simply: 'Today, these words have come true.'

His listeners were amazed at what he said. Then Jesus went on to warn them: 'Believe me, I know that you want me to work miracles here, as you have heard I do in other places. But the long history of our people shows that, time and again, the prophets who speak God's message are rejected in their own town.'

The people gathered around him as an angry mob. They hustled him to a craggy cliff on a hillside outside the town, thinking to hurl him over and there stone him to death.

At the last moment, Jesus turned, walked through the crowd, and went to another place.

The Miracles Begin

Jesus went over the hills and down to Lake Galilee, to a little fishing village called Capernaum. Once again, he spoke to people in the synagogues of the region.

He began to heal people too... With a word or a touch he could cure those who were troubled in body and in mind. Here was news indeed.

People wanted to find out for themselves if the stories were true. One day, after sunset, all who had friends who were sick with various diseases brought them to Jesus; he placed his hands on every one of them and healed them all.

Retold from Luke 4:14–40 and Isaiah 61:1–2

Heal Us All

At even, when the sun was set,
The sick, O Lord, around Thee lay;
O in what diverse pains they met!
O with what joy they went away!

Once more 'tis eventide, and we,
Oppressed with various ills, draw near;
What if thy form we cannot see?
We know and feel that thou art here...

Thy touch has still its ancient power,
No word from thee can fruitless fall;
Hear in this solemn evening hour,
And in thy mercy heal us all.

Henry Twells (1823–1900)

15

Following Jesus

One day, Jesus was standing on the shore of Lake Galilee. A crowd gathered to hear him… eager, anxious. They pressed close around him on all sides. Seeing two fishing boats on the beach, Jesus got into one, and asked the fishermen to push it a little way into the water. From there he continued to teach the people.

Jesus Calls the Fishermen

Jesus spent many hours talking to the crowds from a fishing boat. When he had finished, he spoke to the young fisherman. 'Simon, push your boat out further. Let your net down in the deep water for a catch of fish.'

'It will do no good,' replied Simon Peter. 'We worked hard all night long and caught nothing.'

Jesus looked at him and held his gaze.

'Oh, I'll do it if you ask,' he shrugged.

He and his helper let the nets down, lazily and without interest. But what was this? A sudden pull, a familiar tugging on the ropes… The nets were heavy with fish.

'Come, come quickly and help,' shouted Simon Peter to the men lounging by the second boat. 'Help us, we're sinking!'

Together they struggled, tugging at the heavy nets, glancing fearfully as the water lapped nearer and nearer the top of the boat, so low were they now in the water. They heaved on the oars, and brought their craft to shore.

Safe on land, Simon Peter fell on his knees before Jesus. 'Go away and leave me,' he said. 'Whoever you are, you don't need to have anything to do with the likes of me.' The other men—James and John—did the same.

'Don't be afraid,' replied Jesus. 'You are strong men, all of you: hard-working men who can haul fish from the murky depths of the lake. From now on you'll be working with me, gathering people up from their deep darkness.'

The men pulled the boats onto the shore, left everything, and followed Jesus.

Retold from Luke 5:1–11

Jesus and the Tax Collector

Another day, Jesus went out and saw a tax collector named Levi sitting in his office. (A tax collector was a man who collaborated with the Roman overlords, was most likely a cheat, collecting more than was right, robbing the poor to make himself rich. Who wanted anything to do with a tax collector?)

Jesus went up to him and said, 'Follow me.'

Levi got up, left everything, and followed him.

Then Levi had a big feast in his house for Jesus, and among the guests was a large number of tax collectors and other people of low repute—people associated with gossip and scandal. The religious people known as Pharisees were appalled. For them, eating with wrongdoers such as these was in itself breaking God's Law. They complained to Jesus' disciples. 'Why do you eat and drink with tax collectors and other outcasts?' they asked sneeringly, secretly delighted that Jesus had spoiled his own reputation.

Jesus replied, 'People who are well do not need a doctor, but only those who are sick. I have not come to call respectable people to repent, but outcasts.'

Retold from Luke 5:27–32

Satan's Nest

God in Heaven, you have helped my life to grow like a tree. Now something has happened. Satan, like a bird, has carried in one twig of his own choosing after another. Before I knew it he had built a dwelling place and was living in it. Tonight, my Father, I am throwing out both the bird and the nest.

Anonymous

The Twelve Disciples

Many people followed Jesus, listening to all he said, and learning to live as he taught. From among them he chose twelve to be his special disciples.

The Welcome-home Story

The religious teachers were enraged to see the kind of people
Jesus gathered around him. How dare Jesus welcome sinners!
In answer, Jesus told this story:

The Father and his Two Sons

'There was once a man who had two sons. Together they ran a prosperous farm. Life was comfortable and good.

But the younger son was impatient. He wanted to go his own way in life. One day he shouted his feelings at his father: "I'm fed up with doing what you want. I want a life of my own. I wish you were dead!"

The older man's eyes clouded with sorrow; but he was a kind and generous man. Speedily he arranged for the son's inheritance to be given to him. In no time, the younger son had sold it all for money. Swaggering, he left, a rich man.

He went far away in search of his dreams… a life sparkling with excitement, rich living and extravagant parties.

While he was spending his money like water, scorching summer weather turned the farmlands to dust. The harvest failed. The price of food soared. In no time at all, the young man found that his money was gone.

The only job he could get was minding a herd of pigs. Pigs! All his life he had been brought up to think of them as filthy. He sat on a rock in the hollow they had rooted bare, picking hungrily at the bean pods that were their food.

Suddenly, despair engulfed him. "My father's servants live better than this," he wept; and he knew he had to make a change.

His sorrow was all he had to offer. "Father," he must say, "I have sinned against God and against you. I am no longer fit to be called your son, so treat me as one of your hired workers." The words were right, he was sure, but, as he drew near home, he wondered if his father would listen.

Into his dejected wondering came the sound of running and shouting.

"My son, my son!" There before him was his father, hugging him, kissing him, dancing him back to the house, sending servants off this way and that to prepare a feast, to fetch new clothes,

to welcome him back to his place in the family. "I'd lost my son; it was like he was dead. And he's here… back with us. Let's celebrate!"

The elder son was out in the fields. He heard the noise of partying… the music, the dancing, the laughter, the clapping. He approached in disbelief, and then white-hot anger swept through him. His father came over to him.

"Why are you eating with that filthy scum who disgraced our family?" asked the son. "And why the party? I've been here all this time, working honestly, decently, sensibly. You've never done anything like this for me."

"My son," said the father, "you have been here always, sharing in everything I have. But we must celebrate now, for your brother is back with us, as if from the dead. He was lost and now we've found him." '

Retold from Luke 15:11–32

Dream of a Bird

You ask me,
what did I dream?
I dreamt I became a bird.
You ask me, why did I
want to become a bird?
I really wanted to
have wings.
You ask me,
why did I want wings?
These wings would
help me fly back to
my country.
You ask me,
why did I want to
go back there?

Because I wanted to find
something I missed.
You ask me,
what do I miss?
I miss the place where
I lived as a child.
You ask me,
What was that place
like?
The place was happy,
my family was close
together…
You ask me,
why I am sad?
I'm sad because all
my friends have fathers.
You ask me,
why does this matter?
Because my father
is far away.
I want to fly to him
like a bird.

Written by a Vietnamese
boy, aged 14

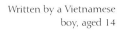

Words of Life

In the villages by Lake Galilee, people had never had so much to talk about. Jesus was turning life upside down. They spread the news of his miracles. They marvelled at his teaching. His words had the ring of truth, and they wanted to remember them always. For some, the message went even further. The words made them want to change the way they lived.

Love Your Enemies

'Love your enemies, do good to those who hate you, bless those who curse you and pray for those who ill-treat you. If anyone hits you on one cheek, let him hit the other one too; if someone takes your coat, let him have your shirt as well. Give to everyone who asks you for something, and when someone takes what is yours, do not ask for it back. Do for others just what you want them to do for you.'

Luke 6:27–31

Do Good in Secret

'When you give something to a needy person, do not make a big show of it, as the hypocrites do in the places of worship and on the streets. They do it so that people will praise them. Getting noticed is all the reward they will get. When you help a needy person, do it in such a way that even your closest friend will not know about it. God will notice, and God will reward you.'

Retold from Matthew 6:2–4

When You Pray

'When you pray, do not make a big show of it, praying where everyone will see you. Go to your room and close the door. Do not use a lot of meaningless words. Simply say this:

Our Father in heaven:

May your holy name be honoured;

May your kingdom come;

May your will be done on earth as it is in heaven.

Give us today the food we need.

Forgive us the wrongs we have done, as we forgive the wrongs that others have done to us.

Do not bring us to hard testing, but keep us safe from the Evil One.'

Retold from Matthew 6:0–13

True Riches

'Do not store up riches for yourselves here on earth, where moths and rust destroy, and robbers break in and steal. Instead, store up riches for yourselves in heaven, where moths and rust cannot destroy, and robbers cannot break in and steal. For your heart will always be where your riches are.'

Matthew 6:19–21

Forgive

'If you forgive others the wrongs they have done to you, your Father in heaven will also forgive you.'

Matthew 6:14

Only let me make my life simple and straight like a flute of reed for Thee to fill with music.'

Anonymous

Lord, make me a channel of your peace.
Where there is hatred, let me sow love,
Where there is injury, pardon,
Where there is doubt, faith,
Where there is despair, hope,
Where there is darkness, light,
Where there is sadness, joy.
O Divine Master, grant that I may not
so much seek to be consoled as to console,
not so much to be understood as to understand,
not so much to be loved as to love;
for it is in giving that we receive,
it is in pardoning that we are pardoned,
it is in dying that we awake to eternal life.

A prayer associated with St Francis of Assisi

A New Kingdom

Jesus had a clear message for all who came to listen to him:
'Give your whole life to living as God's people—as members of God's Kingdom.'
'But what is the Kingdom?' his listeners wanted to know.
Jesus told stories—parables—to explain what the Kingdom is like.

The Great Feast

'There was once a man who was giving a great feast. He invited many people. When it was time for the feast, he sent his servants to call the guests: "Come, everything is ready!"

But one after another, they all began to make excuses…

"I've just bought a field, I must go and look at it," said one.

"I've bought five pairs of oxen, I must go and try them," said another

"I've just got married. I'm sorry, I cannot come," said a third.

When the king heard, he was furious. He said to his servant, "Hurry out to the town, and bring back the poor, the crippled, the blind and the lame who to be found sitting on street corners and in gloomy alleys."

Soon the servant returned and said, "Sir, we have carried out your order, but there is still room at your feast."

So the king said, "Go out into the countryside, seeking people far and wide, so that my house will be full. I tell you, none of those who refused the invitation will taste my feast." '

Retold from Luke 14:16–24

The Mustard Seed

'The kingdom of heaven is like this...
A man takes a mustard seed and sows it
on his land. The mustard seed is just a
tiny thing, but it grows into a huge
plant. It becomes a tree, and all the
birds come and make their nests in
its branches.'

Retold from Matthew 13:31

The Pearl of Great Price

'The kingdom of heaven is like this...
A man is a collector of fine pearls. One
day, he is shown the most perfect and
exquisite pearl he has ever seen. He goes
and sells all his other possessions. Then
he comes and buys that pearl.'

Retold from Matthew 13:45–46

Let the Children Come

Some people brought their babies to Jesus
for him to place his hands on them. The
disciples saw them, and told them off for
doing so. But Jesus called the children to
him and said, 'Let the children come to me
and do not stop them, because the Kingdom
of God belongs to such as these. Remember
this: whoever does not receive the Kingdom
of God like a child will never enter it.'

Luke 18:15–17

I am only a spark. Make me a fire.
I am only a string. Make me a lyre.
I am only a drop. Make me a fountain.
I am only an ant-hill. Make me a mountain.
I am only a feather. Make me a wing.
I am only a rag. Make me a king!

Source unknown (Mexico)

Living in the Kingdom

Jesus' teaching was fresh and exciting. Ordinary people caught the vision of living full and happy lives. But what did Jesus think of the faith he had been raised in? What of the cherished Law in the scriptures of his own people?

The Greatest Commandment

One day, a teacher of the Law stepped up to Jesus to ask a question. 'Teacher,' he asked Jesus ingratiatingly, 'tell me, what must I do to inherit eternal life?'

'I expect you can answer that well enough,' Jesus smiled. 'What do the scriptures say?'

The man answered, ' "Love the Lord your God with all your heart, with all your soul, with all your strength, and with all your mind" and "Love your neighbour as you love yourself." '

'You know all the right answers yourself,' replied Jesus. 'Do that, and you will live.'

But the man was not going to be dismissed so easily. 'Who is my neighbour?' he persisted.

Jesus answered with a story:

The Good Samaritan

'There was once a man who had to travel from Jerusalem to Jericho.'

Jesus' listeners could picture that dusty road, winding down from the heights of Jerusalem through barren hills that were deeply cut with ravines and gullies. It was empty, wild country… a home to bandits.

Jesus continued: 'As he journeyed, robbers attacked him, stripped him of all he had, beat him up and left him half dead in the road.

Soon, another traveller came by: a priest from the Temple in Jerusalem. Yet when he saw the man, he simply looked away and passed by on the other side.'

The teacher of the Law gasped in protest. There were good reasons why a priest might not stop... the risk of attack, the fact that a wounded man was unclean and a priest shouldn't touch such things...

'That's not the end of the story,' continued Jesus. 'Another man came by. A Levite—a helper in the same Temple. He came over and looked at the man. And then, he too passed by. The traveller who came along next was only a Samaritan.'

Jesus' listeners set their faces into a frown. They were Jews, and they despised the Samaritans. Samaritans did not worship God in the right way.

Jesus continued his story: 'The Samaritan saw the man. He came over, looked at him, and was filled with pity for him. He cleaned the man's wounds and bandaged them. He lifted the man onto his donkey. He took him to an inn. There he asked the innkeeper to take care of the man, and gave him the money to pay for it. "I'll be coming back this way soon," he said. "If there is more to pay for this man, you shall have it then." '

Jesus looked steadily at the teacher of Law. 'What is your opinion?' he asked. 'Which of these men acted like a neighbour to the man attacked by robbers?'

'The one who was kind to him,' said the man.

Jesus replied, 'You go then, and do the same.'

Retold from Luke 10:25–37

Lord Jesus,
I give thee my hands
to do thy work.
I give thee my feet
to go thy way.
I give thee my eyes
to see as thou seest.
I give thee my tongue
to speak thy words.
I give thee my mind
that thou mayest think in me.
I give thee my spirit
that thou mayest pray in me.
Above all, I give thee my heart
that thou mayest love in me thy
Father, and all mankind.
I give thee my whole self
that thou mayest grow in me, so
that it is thee, Lord Jesus, who
live and work and pray in me.

Lancelot Andrewes (1555–1626)

A Message of Life

*Jesus told people that those who followed him would
have a rich reward: life in all its fullness.*

Walking With God

*Alas, my God, that we should be
Such strangers to each other!
O that as friends we might agree,
And walk and talk together!*

Thomas Shepherd (1665–1739)

Life-giving Water

Noontime in Samaria. The sun beat down,
fierce and hot. Jesus sat by a well. A drink
would be so welcome as he travelled. A woman
came along to draw water.

'Please give me a drink,' he asked.

She turned in surprise. 'You're a Jew,' she
replied curtly. 'I'm a Samaritan. Your Law says
you can't share the same cup as me.'

Jesus replied, 'If only you knew what God
gives, and who it is that is asking you for a
drink, you would be the one asking for a drink:
a drink of life-giving water.'

Then he told her about her life… the
friendships that had all gone wrong, the shame
of being a woman with a string of lovers and no
one who called her his wife. Yet he did not
condemn her.

He talked about the rift between Jews and
Samaritans, arguing about the right place to
worship God. 'The time is coming,' he said,
'when it won't matter where people go to
worship God. Everyone will be able to worship
God as God is.'

The woman said, 'I know that one day God's
Messiah will come, and he will tell us everything
about living as God's people.'

Jesus answered, 'I am he, who is talking
with you.'

The woman was convinced. She gathered
everyone she knew to come and listen to Jesus
who told them that it did not matter how much
the religious people of Jerusalem sneered
at them. They too could be God's people.

Retold from John 4:5–30

Life-giving Food

One day, Jesus and his disciples took one of their boats across Lake Galilee. A huge crowd followed them, eager to see Jesus' miracles.

Jesus looked at the crowds on the hillside below him. 'Where can we buy food to feed them all?' he asked one of the disciples.

'Think first of the cost,' gasped the man. 'It would be more than half a year's wages.'

Another spoke up: 'There is a boy here who has five loaves of barley bread and two fish. But that won't be enough for this crowd.'

It was a grassy spot, and Jesus asked his disciples to make the people sit down.

Jesus took the bread, and gave thanks to God. Then he handed it out to the people.

He did the same with the fish.

People passed the food from one to another, and there was always a piece left to pass on.

Miraculously, there was enough for everyone.

When the people had eaten all they wanted, Jesus asked his disciples to gather the scraps. There were enough to fill twelve baskets.

That night, Jesus' disciples got into a boat and went back across the lake. Night came, and a strong wind began to blow. Suddenly, the disciples saw Jesus walking on the water, coming towards them. They were terrified.

'Don't be afraid,' said Jesus. 'It is I.'

The men helped Jesus into the boat… and immediately they reached the place they were heading for.

The next day, the people came looking for Jesus again.

'You are looking for me because you ate the bread yesterday,' said Jesus, 'but you didn't understand the miracle. Do not work for food that goes bad; instead, work for the bread that lasts for eternal life.'

'Give us that bread!' came the shout.

'I am the bread of life,' Jesus told them. 'The person who comes to me will never be hungry, never be thirsty.'

Retold from John 0:1–35

The Light of Life

Nicodemus was a Pharisee. Many of his friends despised Jesus, but Nicodemus had heard of his teaching, and of his healing, and he wanted an answer to a question. So he arranged a special night-time meeting with Jesus and asked, 'Jesus, are you really a teacher sent by God? No one could do the miracles you do unless God was with them.'

Jesus told him that he would never understand about God and God's Kingdom unless he let God change him and the way he saw the world. It would be like becoming a new person—like being born again!

The Light That Shines

Nicodemus listened intently to Jesus. The old man had been a religious teacher all his life, yet what Jesus had to say about God seemed to make sense of everything.

'The light has come into the world,' explained Jesus, 'but people love the darkness rather than the light, because the things they do are evil. Anyone who does evil things hates the light and will not come to the light, because they don't want their evil deeds to be shown up. But whoever does what is true comes to the light in order that the light may show that what they did was in obedience to God.'

Retold from John 3:19–21

The Light of the World

On another occasion, Jesus said, 'I am the light of the world. Whoever follows me will have the light of life and will never walk in darkness.'

Retold from John 8:12

The Blind Man

One day, as Jesus was walking along, he saw a man begging by the roadside. He had been born blind: never able to enjoy the violet dawn light nor the amber evening; never able to labour for his living in the blue and gold noontime. His parents had had to look after him always. They still looked after him, but as they grew frailer and could not work, their son had to beg for a living.

'Just look at that man!' exclaimed one of Jesus' followers.

'I wonder why God lets such misfortune fall upon some people and not others,' added another. 'What do you think, Jesus? Do you think bad things happened to him because he's a bad person. Or should we blame his parents?'

'Neither,' said Jesus. 'He is blind so that we can see God's power to heal. That's what I'm here for: to show God's power to people; to be light in this dark world for as long as I am in it.'

Then Jesus made a paste from mud and his own spit, put it on the man's eyes, and told him to go and wash in a pool of water nearby.

He did so. And as he washed the sticky paste from his face… Oh miracle! Oh wonder! Before his eyes was a dazzle of brightness and colour. 'I can see!' he shouted, 'I can see!'

People stared. They rubbed their own eyes and blinked, suddenly unable to trust their own eyes. 'He says he can see,' they whispered. 'He says he can see God's own daylight.'

When the Pharisees heard of this, they were angry. 'This is serious news,' they said sourly. 'This so-called healing took place on the sabbath. Then this Jesus simply cannot be from God, for he does not obey God's sabbath law. He is a sinner.'

'But how does he heal people if he is not from God?' asked some. And they began to argue.

Finally, to settle their quarrelling they questioned the man who had been given his sight. 'I don't know if he is a sinner or not,' said the man. 'All I know is this: I once was blind, and now I can see.'

Retold from John 9:1–25

Lord Jesus, you are my light
In the darkness,
You are my warmth
In the cold,
You are my happiness
In sorrow…

Anonymous

The Shepherd and the Sheep

The religious men were arguing. Tempers were rising.

'Just look at the following Jesus has,' argued one. 'There must be something in what he says if so many believe in him.'

'Fool,' sneered another. 'The crowds are just uneducated. They don't know the Law as explained in our scriptures. They don't have the knowledge about God to see that Jesus is an imposter—pretending to be the Messiah.'

'And the scriptures are clear on one thing,' added another, 'no prophet ever comes from Galilee. So how could Jesus of Nazareth be a prophet, let alone the Messiah?'

'Jesus says that if we reject him, we are rejecting God. I do not want to reject God—and by whose power does he work those miracles of healing? That blind man he healed was blind from birth, yet now he really can see.'

'Perhaps we're the ones who are blind,' added another sadly. 'Perhaps we are blind to God's messenger.'

Retold from John 7 and 9

The Good Shepherd

While the religious people were arguing about Jesus and his following, Jesus was out on the hillside, where a shepherd was leading his flock out of the safety of a stone-walled sheepfold and going in search of pasture for his animals.

Jesus watched him and began speaking to the crowd. 'The person who doesn't go into a sheepfold through the gate is a thief and a robber. The man who goes in through the gate is the shepherd. The gatekeeper opens the gate for him; the sheep hear his voice as he calls his own sheep by name, and he leads them out.

Then he goes ahead of them, and the sheep follow him, because they know his voice. They will not follow someone else—rather, they will run away from any other person.'

And Jesus continued, 'I am the gate for the sheep. All the other people who came before me and claimed to be leading people to God were thieves and robbers. People didn't listen to them.

I am the gate: whoever comes to God through me will be safe. That person will go in and come out and find pasture. The thief only comes to kill and destroy. I have come in order that you may have life—life in all its fullness.

I am the good shepherd, who is willing to die for the sheep. When the hired man sees a wolf coming to his flock, he runs away and the sheep are scattered. He has no care for the sheep. But just as I know my Father and my Father knows me, so I know my sheep and they know me. I am gathering together one great flock, and I will lead them to life.'

Retold from John 10:1–16

God's Ancient Promise

'I, the Lord, tell you you that I myself will look for my sheep and take care of them in the same way as a shepherd takes care of his sheep that were scattered and are brought together again.'

Ezekiel 34:11–12

A Shepherd Boy's Song

The Lord's my shepherd, I'll not want;
He makes me down to lie
In pastures green; he leadeth me
The quiet waters by.

My soul he doth restore again,
And me to walk doth make
Within the paths of righteousness,
E'en for his own name's sake.

Yea, though I walk in death's dark vale,
Yet will I fear no ill:
For thou art with me, and thy rod
And staff me comfort still…

Goodness and mercy all my life
Shall surely follow me;
And in God's house for evermore
My dwelling-place shall be.

Psalm 23
(Scottish Psalter 1650)

A Children's Hymn

Loving shepherd of thy sheep,
Keep thy lamb, in safety keep;
Nothing can thy power withstand,
None can pluck me from thy hand.

Jane E. Leeson (1807–82)

The Miracle of Life

An eastward road out of Jerusalem twists and turns its way among olive-clad hills and soon brings the traveller to a village named Bethany.

There lived a man named Lazarus, with his sisters Martha and Mary. All three were friends of Jesus.

The Death of Lazarus

One day, Lazarus fell ill, and his sisters feared for his life. They sent a message to Jesus: 'Lord, your dear friend is ill.'

When Jesus heard the message, he said to those around him, 'The end of this illness will not be the death of Lazarus, but glory to God and God's son.'

But although the message itself had taken some time to arrive, Jesus made no move to go back to Bethany for two more days. When he and his disciples reached Bethany, they found that Lazarus had been buried four days earlier. Many people had come out from Jerusalem to mourn with the two sisters.

When Martha heard that Jesus was coming, she went out to meet him. Mary stayed in the house.

Martha's face was pale with weeping as she walked up to Jesus and spoke to him. 'If you had been here, Lord, my brother would not have died!' she said. 'But I know that even now God will give you whatever you ask him for.'

'Your brother will rise to life,' Jesus told her.

'I know that he will rise to life on the last day,' she replied.

Jesus said to her, 'I am the resurrection and the life. Whoever believes in me will live, even though he dies; and whoever lives and believes in me will never die. Do you believe this?'

'Yes,' replied Martha. 'I do believe that you are the Messiah, the Son of God, who was to come into the world.'

They walked closer to the village, and Martha went ahead to tell Mary of Jesus' arrival. He came and saw all the people weeping.

'Where have you buried him?' he asked.

'Come and see,' they replied.

When Jesus reached the tomb—a cave with a round stone door—he wept. He was weeping for sorrow at the loss of his friend.

Then, to everyone's amazement, Jesus said, 'Take the stone away.'

Martha was horrified: 'We dare not do that. There will be a bad smell. My brother has been dead four days.'

Jesus said, 'Didn't I tell you that you would see God's glory if you believed?'

Hesitant, uncertain, curious, excited: the crowd of mourners watched as strong people heaved the stone door open.

Jesus said a prayer to God. Then he called in a loud voice, 'Lazarus, come out!'

Lazarus came walking from the tomb.

Retold from John 11:1–44

Kindly spring again is here,
Trees and fields in bloom appear;
Hark! the birds with artless lays
Warble their creator's praise.

Where in winter all was snow,
Now the flowers in clusters grow;
And the corn, in green array,
Promises a harvest-day.

Lord, afford a spring to me,
Let me feel like what I see;
Speak, and by thy gracious voice,
Make my drooping soul rejoice.

On thy garden deign to smile,
Raise the plants, enrich the soil;
Soon thy presence will restore
Life to what seemed dead before.

John Newton (1725–1807)

The Great Welcome

Jesus and his friends were now very close to Jerusalem. Pilgrims from all over the world were travelling there, for it was time to celebrate the Passover festival.

God Bless the King of Israel!

The news spread through all Jerusalem that Jesus was coming, and excitement shimmered in the air. Here was the man who had raised a dead man to life. What other wonders might he work? Everyone wanted to know…

Already some could see him—on the road that wound its way down the Mount of Olives, just outside the city walls. He was riding a donkey.

This was news indeed! The scriptures said that the nation's king would come riding a donkey. Jesus must be that king! Here was the one who was going to rescue his people!

Some people could remember the actual words from the book of the prophet Zechariah:

'Rejoice, rejoice, people of Zion!
Shout for joy, you people of Jerusalem!
Look, your king is coming to you!
He comes triumphant and victorious,
but humble and riding on a donkey—
on a colt, the foal of a donkey…
When that day comes, the Lord will save
his people,

as a shepherd saves his flock from danger.
They will shine in his land
like the jewels of a crown.
How good and beautiful the land will be!'

Men tugged at the spiky palm trees that lined the road and ripped off great branches. They danced and sang their way to greet Jesus, waving their leafy banners.

'Praise God!' came the shout.

'God bless the king who comes in the name of the Lord!'

'God bless the king of Israel!'

Soon everyone on the road was joining with them: men and women were shouting, singing and clapping; children were dancing, and old people who struggled to walk with a stick swayed to the same joyful rhythm; wealthy people in new clothes bought for the pilgrimage laughed for joy, along with beggars from Jerusalem in their rags. The tumult rang from the bottom of the valley to the surrounding hilltops… even the hilltop where the Temple stood.

The Gathering Storm

And yet, amidst the sunshine and the joy, trouble lurked… All around, enemies were gathering, whispering, plotting, scheming. A dark cloud of hatred hung over them.

'You see,' muttered the Pharisees. 'We are not succeeding at all in putting down this man's madness. Look! The whole world is following him!'

Retold from John 12:12–19 and Zechariah 9:9, 16–17

Love Unknown

My song is love unknown,
My Saviour's love to me,
Love to the loveless shown,
That they might lovely be.
O, who am I,
That for my sake
My Lord should take
Frail flesh, and die?…

Sometimes they strew his way,
And his sweet praises sing;
Resounding all the day
Hosannas to their King.
Then 'Crucify!'
Is all their breath,
And for his death
They thirst and cry.

Why, what hath my Lord done?
What makes this rage and spite?
He made the lame to run,
He gave the blind their sight.
Sweet injuries!
Yet they at these
Themselves displease
And 'gainst him rise.

They rise, and needs will have
My dear Lord made away;
A murderer they save,
The Prince of Life they slay.
Yet cheerful he
To suffering goes,
That he his foes
From thence might free.

Samuel Crossman (1624–83)

Celebration Into Sorrow

Jesus and his followers were in Jerusalem preparing to celebrate the Passover.
They were going to share one of the special Passover meals together.

A New Commandment

It was nearly time to begin the festival meal. This should have been a time of joy and celebration, but already Jesus knew that his enemies were ready to close in on him, and that their plan was to kill him. He was very sad.

To his friends' surprise, he got up from the table, took off his outer garment and tied a towel round his waist. Then he poured water into a basin. Like a household slave, he was offering to wash his companions' feet. They were very surprised.

'This isn't the kind of work you should be doing,' protested Peter.

'You must let me,' said Jesus. 'You will understand why later.'

After Jesus had washed their feet he took his place at the table again and began to explain:

'You call me your teacher; you call me your master; and that is what I am. Yet I have washed your feet. It is an example for you to follow: you must do humble tasks like this for one another.'

As the evening wore on, he gave another reminder. 'Listen,' he said, 'I am giving you a new commandment: you must love one another. As I have loved you, so you must love one another.'

Retold from John 13:1–16, 34

The Last Supper

While they were sitting down to eat, Jesus said, 'You have all been my close companions and followers. But already I know that one of you is going to betray me.'

They were shocked, and began to protest loudly.

'Surely it's not me?' said one.

'I would never do that!' exclaimed another.

'Impossible!'

And they all denied that they would ever do such a thing.

Jesus did not argue; nor did he change his mind. So they continued the meal. It was a Passover, after all: a time to remember the story behind the festival…

The story told of a time, a thousand years earlier, when God had rescued them from slavery in Egypt and led them to a land they could make their home. God had made a covenant with the nation: a special promise to be their God, and for them to be God's people.

They were following the old traditions when Jesus did something different. He took a piece of bread and broke it, and gave it to his companions. 'Take and eat it,' he said, 'this is

my body.' Then he took the cup of wine, and gave thanks to God. 'Drink this, all of you,' he said, 'this is my blood. It is the seal of God's new covenant—the sign that you can trust in God's new promise. My blood is going to be poured out for the forgiveness of sins. I will never again drink this wine until the day I drink the new wine with you in my Father's Kingdom.'

What he said was puzzling… disturbing, even. But then, Jesus often said things that left them wondering what to make of it all. So they let it pass.

After the meal they sang a hymn and they all went out into the night. All? Where was Judas? He looked after the money. Had he gone to buy something at Jesus' request? He must be on some errand.

Retold from Matthew 26:20–30 and John 13:21–30

Gethsemane

They went together to an olive grove called Gethsemane, just outside Jerusalem. There, among the gaunt and twisted shapes of the ancient trees, Jesus prayed and Jesus wept.

Retold from Matthew 26:30–46

Weep yet awhile,—
Weep till that day shall dawn
when thou shalt smile:
Watch till the day
When all save only love shall pass away.

Christina Rossetti (1830–94)

The Way to the Cross

Sometimes Jesus seemed to have many friends.
Now his enemies were to show their strength.

Betrayed and Tried

Jesus was praying among the olive trees. His companions were asleep.

Suddenly came a blaze of light: lanterns… torches… the sound of iron weapons…

Judas came up and greeted Jesus with a kiss. Behind him were armed men. Jesus remained calm. He did not fight. He let the soldiers take him away. His companions ran away in terror.

The guards took Jesus to the religious leaders. They asked questions. Who were his followers? What was he teaching them?

Jesus answered, 'I have always spoken publicly to everyone; all my teaching was done in the synagogues and in the Temple. I have never said anything in secret. Why, then, do you question me? Question the people who heard me.'

This answer only made them angry. They slapped Jesus and hit him, and in the morning they handed him over to the Roman governor, Pontius Pilate.

Pilate had little interest in Jesus. There were plenty of young men in this province keen to lead their people to freedom. Jesus was like them… only he wasn't a fighter. 'Are you the king of the Jews, as your enemies claim you say you are?' he enquired.

Jesus replied, 'My kingdom does not belong to this world. If it did, my followers would fight to keep me safe from my enemies. No: I was born and came into the world for one purpose—to speak about the truth. Whoever belongs to the truth listens to me.'

Pilate wanted to set Jesus free; but how could

he do so and still please the people? It was the custom at this festival time for him to set a prisoner free, so he decided to appeal to the crowds. From a high platform of his palace he spoke to the people: 'Do you want me to set free for you the King of the Jews?' he called.

A few days earlier, crowds had welcomed Jesus. But Jesus' enemies had been hard at work. 'Crucify him, crucify him,' came the clamour. Pilate saw that his plan had failed, and now he feared a riot. Washing his hands of the case, he let Jesus' own people have their way.

Retold from John 18—19:16

Crucified

Roman soldiers did the terrible work of crucifixion. They nailed living flesh to rough wood, and hoisted the cross up on a hillside for all to see.

Jesus was in anguish. He was dying. It seemed his life's work had failed. He cried aloud two lines from a psalm he had learned when he was a boy: 'My God, my God, why have you abandoned me?'

No help came. The sky grew dark with an eclipse. The hours wore on. Jesus saw his mother standing with his friend John, and he called to them, asking the young man to take care of the old and sorrowing Mary. He looked down at all the people... his triumphant enemies, his frightened weeping friends, and he said a prayer to God: 'Father, forgive them. They don't know what they are doing.'

Retold from Mark 15:33–41, John 19:17–31 and Luke 23:20–34

A Tree that Became a Cross

Many years ago—the memory abides—
I was felled to the ground at the forest's edge,
Severed from my roots. Enemies seized me,
Made of me a mark of scorn for criminals to
mount on...
I was raised up a Rood, a royal King I bore,
The High King of Heaven: hold firm I must.
They drove dark nails through me, the dire wounds
still show,
Cruel gaping gashes, yet I dared not give as good.
They taunted the two of us; I was wet with teeming
blood,
Streaming from the warrior's side when he sent
forth his spirit.
High upon that hill helpless I suffered
Long hours of torment; I saw the Lord of Hosts
Outstretched in agony; all-embracing darkness
Covered with thick clouds the corpse of the World's
Ruler;
The bright day was darkened by a deep shadow,
All its colours clouded; the whole creation wept,
Keened for its King's fall; Christ was on the Rood.

Anonymous
From 'The Dream of the Rood'

Buried

That night, some of Jesus' friends came to take away his broken body and lay it in a tomb. The sun was setting: the sabbath day of rest was beginning. So they rolled the stone door of the tomb shut, and went away.

Retold from Mark 15:42–47

Miracle Morning

*Jesus was buried just as the sun was setting, when the sabbath day of rest
was beginning. The sabbath passed: a sabbath without Jesus,
a sabbath of grief and mourning. Then another day dawned.*

In the Garden

Jesus was dead. No one felt the pain of loss more keenly than the one they called Mary Magdalene. She remembered the old days before she met Jesus—her wild life, her wild temper, her wild hatred. Jesus had been a friend unlike any other. He had helped her to change, to become the person she had dreamt of being.

Now weeping, she returned to the tomb with a group of women while the sky was still dark.

As Mary drew nearer and could make out the shapes of the objects around it, her heart lurched. The stone was rolled back. The tomb was open. Someone had been there already. Fear and terror chilled her.

And then she ran—she needed help, and quickly. Simon Peter and John, Jesus' friends—they needed to know. They needed to do something. 'They have taken Jesus from the tomb!' she cried. 'We don't know where they have taken him.' The two men leaped up and raced to the tomb... John reached the mouth of the cave and stopped in amazement.

Peter rushed on... there were the cloths used to wrap the body; they were empty. Jesus had gone from the tomb. They looked around, wild-eyed. Was this a trap? Could this event have a simple, reasonable explanation? But there were no clues to be found, so they went away.

Mary stood behind, weeping. Tears dimmed her eyes. Why was the body not in the tomb? Perhaps if she looked again it would all be different.

Then she saw them... two figures dressed in shining white... angels. 'Woman, why are you crying?' they asked.

'They have taken my Lord away,' she wept, 'and I do not know where they have put him.'

She turned around. A man was passing. He asked the same question: 'Why are you crying? Who are you looking for?'

Mary thought it must be the man who tended the little grove. Perhaps he had seen what happened.

'Oh, if you have taken Jesus' body, please tell me where it is and I will go and get him,' she begged.

'Mary,' said the man.

Then she knew. It was Jesus.

He was alive.

Retold from John 20:1–16

When Mary Thro' the Garden Went

When Mary thro' the garden went
There was no sound of any bird,
And yet, because the night was spent,
The little grasses lightly stirred,
The flowers awoke, the lilies heard.

When Mary thro' the garden went
The dew lay still on flower and grass,
The waving palms about her sent
Their fragrance out as she did pass,
No light upon the branches was.

When Mary thro' the garden went,
Her eyes, for weeping long, were dim,
The grass beneath her footsteps bent,
The solemn lilies, white and slim,
These also stood and wept for him.

When Mary thro' the garden went,
She sought, within the garden ground,
One for whom her heart was rent,
One who for her sake was bound,
One who sought and she was found.

Mary Coleridge (1861–1907)

Spring bursts today,
For Christ is risen and all the earth's
at play…

Sing, Creatures, sing,
Angels and Men and Birds and
everything.

All notes of Doves
Fill all our world: this is the time
of loves.

Christina Rossetti (1830–94)

New Life

It was late that Sunday evening… the first Sunday after Jesus' crucifixion.

The Disciples' Story

Jesus' closest friends had gathered together again. They had locked the doors securely. Fear made them cautious: the powerful people who had arranged for Jesus' execution might seek them out too.

They were not only fearful. They were still grieving for their dear friend Jesus, so recently put to death; and they were also in turmoil at the news that his body was gone, unsure what to make of the stories they were hearing.

Then Jesus came and stood among them. 'Peace be with you,' he said. Then he showed them the marks in his hands and his side where the soldiers had wounded him.

So the rumours were true! They could see for themselves. Jesus was really alive! Joy flooded over them.

Thomas' Story

The disciple named Thomas had not been with the others when Jesus appeared. When he returned, he could not believe what they were saying. 'Let me see Jesus for myself,' he said angrily; 'let me touch his scarred hands. Unless I do, I will not believe.'

The days passed; for Thomas, they were days of doubting, wondering: 'Surely it can't be true. Surely my companions were dreaming. Yet they seem so sure. They all tell me the same story.'

They talked endlessly together, remembering the things Jesus had said, trying to make sense of it all…

Retold from John 20:19–25

Remembering: the Vine

'I am the vine and you are the branches,' Jesus
had said. 'As long as you remain joined to me,
you will bear fruit in all you do—you will do great
things for God. If you abandon me, you will
achieve nothing. I love you just as the Father
loves me… Remain in my love… do the things
I have told you to do… love one another…'

· The disciples looked at the new season's vine
branches growing strongly and wondered…

Retold from John 15:5–17

Thomas' Story Continues

A week later, the friends were together
again and still they kept the doors locked.
On this occasion, Thomas was with them.

Once again, Jesus came and stood among
them and said, 'Peace be with you.'

Then he spoke to Thomas: 'Here are my
wounded hands, my wounded side. Touch
them, and believe I am here.'

Thomas replied, 'My Lord and my God!'

Retold from John 20:20–28

Wilt thou not visit me?
The plant beside me feels thy gentle dew,
And every blade of grass I see
From thy deep earth its quickening moisture drew.

Wilt thou not visit me?
Thy morning calls on me with cheering tone;
And every hill and tree
Lend but one voice—the voice of thee alone.

Come, for I need thy love,
More than the flower the dew or grass the rain;
Come, gently as thy holy dove;
And let me in thy sight rejoice to live again.

I will not hide from them
When thy storms come, though fierce may be their wrath,
But bow with leafy stem,
And strengthened follow on thy chosen path.

Yes, thou wilt visit me:
Nor plant nor tree thine eye delights so well,
As, when from sin set free,
My spirit loves with thine in peace to dwell.

Jones Very (1813–80)

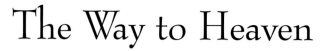

The Way to Heaven

The days went by. More and more people claimed to have seen Jesus. They said he had shared meals with them. They said he had spoken to them at length and he had told them that his dying on a cross was all part of what had to happen.

He had explained that people had turned away from God. They had wanted to go their own way. They had fallen into wrongdoing. They had brought upon themselves great sadness.

Jesus had come to meet them in their sorrow; to suffer with them. He had come to die at their hands, taking upon himself all the bitterness of their wrongdoing.

But death could not hold him. He had risen to new life, and opened up a pathway to life with God. Those who chose to travel that road would find joy in this world and their journey would take them to heaven.

Retold from Luke 24

The Way

Before he died, Jesus had warned his disciples of what was to come.

'I will not be with you much longer… and where I am going you cannot follow.

But do not be worried or upset. Believe in God and believe in me. There are many rooms in my Father's house, and I am going to prepare a place for you… You know the way that leads to the place where I am going.'

Thomas had protested. 'We don't know where you are going, so how can we know how to get there?'

Jesus replied, 'I am the way, the truth and the life. I am the only way to the Father… the only way to God.'

Retold from John 13:36—14:6

Meet With Us

Jesus our Master,
meet us while we walk in the way,
longing to reach your country.
So that following your light,
we may keep the way of righteousness,
and never wander away
into the horrible darkness of this world's night,
while you,
who are the Way, the Truth and the Life,
are shining within us.

From The Gelasian Sacramentary

Blessed

For whom would God do good and great and wonderful things? Jesus had told his followers the answer many times. Now it made more sense:

'Blessed are you poor: the Kingdom of God is yours!

Blessed are you who are hungry now; you will be filled!

Blessed are you who weep now; you will laugh!

Blessed are you when people hate you, reject you, insult you, and say that you are evil, all because of the Son of Man! Be glad when that happens, and dance for joy, because a great reward is kept for you in heaven.'

Retold from Luke 6:20–23

Uphill

Does the road wind uphill all the way?
Yes, to the very end.
Will the day's journey take the whole long day?
From morn to night, my friend.

But is there for the night a resting-place?
A roof for when the slow, dark hours begin.
May not the darkness hide it from my face?
You cannot miss that inn.

Shall I meet other wayfarers at night?
Those who have gone before.
Then must I knock, or call when just in sight?
They will not keep you waiting at that door.

Shall I find comfort, travel-sore and weak?
Of labour you shall find the sum.
Will there be beds for me and all who seek?
Yes, beds for all who come.

Christina Rossetti (1830–94)

A Helper on the Way

Forty days had passed since Mary had found the empty tomb. Jesus had
appeared to his followers many times. They were now sure he was alive.
'Stay here in Jerusalem,' he said. 'Remember the promise I made: God will give you a
helper to strengthen you in the work of spreading my message to all the world.'

Retold from Acts 1:3–8

The Promise

Jesus had made this promise:

'Whoever loves me will obey my teaching. My Father will love that person. My Father and I will come and live with them…

The Helper, the Holy Spirit, whom the Father will send in my name, will teach you everything and make you remember all that I have told you.'

John 14:23, 26

Christ be with me, Christ within me,
Christ behind me, Christ before me,
Christ beside me, Christ to win me,
Christ to comfort and restore me,
Christ beneath me, Christ above me,
Christ in quiet, Christ in danger,
Christ in hearts of all that love me,
Christ in mouth of friend and stranger.

St Patrick (385–461)

Jesus' Farewell

Jesus led his close companions a short way out of Jerusalem. He raised his hands and blessed them. As he did so, he was taken up into heaven.

Ten days later came the Jewish festival called Pentecost. The disciples were all gathered together. Suddenly, there was a noise from the sky. It sounded like a strong wind, and it filled the house where they were sitting. Then it seemed as if tongues of flame spread out and touched each person there. Suddenly, they knew they could do things they had never been able to do before: they had new strength to tell the whole world about Jesus, for Jesus was with them in this new way for always.

They went out into the streets of Jerusalem with a message for the people there… a message about Jesus to spread to the furthest corner of the world.

Retold from Acts 1:9, 2:1–4

It is a flame of fire from midmost heaven that came down hither into the world, fire that will kindle my stubborn nature, fire that will fill my whole life; it will not fail while God remains in being.

I shall never be able to declare, if I should try as long as I live, how pleasant, how sweet, how strong his love is: it is an endless flame that came from midmost heaven to earth.

Thou hast kindled fire in me—the most perfect fire of heaven, which the great seas cannot quench at all.

O a passionate, powerful strong flame of fire has been kindled in heaven; everlasting love it is, that has made a union between God and me.

Source unknown

Index